Eggs of Hope

Inspirational Pysanky Tales of Bravery and Resilience in the Face of Adversity

by Pysanky Publishing

"The air was thick with the stench of death and despair. The women in the Nazi concentration camp huddled together, their spirits broken by the cruelty of their captors. But in the depths of their sorrow, a small glimmer of hope shone through..."

Acknowledgments

We thank all of the editors, researchers, and contributors who made it possible for us to publish this collection of short pysanky stories. Your commitment, effort, and knowledge have significantly raised the calibre of this publication. Also, we are appreciative of our readers' interest in our initiative as well as the support of our families and other loved ones.

Contents

Introduction: The Art & Tradition of Pysanky

Greetings, fellow art enthusiasts! Are you ready to learn about an ancient Ukrainian tradition that's more than just a decorative art form? I'm talking about pysanky - the intricate designs on these eggs hold a world of cultural and spiritual significance that have inspired hope, resilience, and bravery in times of adversity for centuries.

Pysanky are not just art, they're a living connection to Ukrainian culture and history. Each design is carefully made with wax and dyes, and the symbols used represent the natural world, animals, and geometric patterns. Each symbol has its own meaning and purpose.

But the story of pysanky goes beyond its aesthetic appeal. It represents the unwavering spirit of the Ukrainian people, who have faced numerous challenges throughout history, yet have remained steadfast in their cultural identity. Pysanky have been used as protection charms, fertility charms, and signs of hope during hard times.

In fact, during the 2014 Ukrainian Revolution, pysanky became powerful symbols of resistance and unity for protesters who carried them as they fought for a better future.

This book of 10 short stories dives deep into the rich history and cultural significance of pysanky. You'll discover how these intricate designs have touched the lives of people from all walks of life, inspiring them to find courage and hope in times of adversity.

So, join us on this journey through Ukrainian history and immerse yourself in the world of pysanky. These stories will uplift and inspire you, showing you the true power of art to bring hope, resilience, and bravery in the face of adversity. Let's explore the magic of pysanky together!

Unlocking the Magic of Pysanky - A Quick DIY Guide

So what are pysanky, and how exactly do you make them? Beeswax and dyes are used to make intricate designs on eggs, which is a traditional Ukrainian art. The designs are made with a beeswax-filled stylus or kistka. This creates a barrier that keeps the dye from getting into the eggshell. The result is a beautiful and unique work of art that carries deep cultural and spiritual significance.

To get started, you'll need a few materials, including raw eggs, beeswax, a stylus or kistka, dye, and paper towels or cloth for wiping off excess wax. Once you have these materials, you're ready to begin the process of creating your own pysanky.

The first step is to clean and prepare the eggs. Wash them with warm water and mild soap and let them dry. Then, use a small needle to poke a hole in both ends of the egg and blow out the contents. Be careful not to crack the egg!

Next, draw your design on the egg using the stylus or kistka filled with beeswax. Start with the lightest colors first, and then move on to

darker colors. The wax will make a barrier that keeps the dye from getting into the eggshell. Once the wax is taken off, the design will be visible.

After putting the wax design on the egg, dip it for a few minutes in the lightest color dye until you get the color you want. Be sure to wipe off the excess dye with a paper towel or cloth. Then, add more wax to areas that need to remain white or light, and immerse the egg in the next color dye. Repeat the process until all colors have been added.

Once the final color has been applied, it's time to remove the wax. Hold the egg near a flame to melt the wax, and then wipe it off with a paper towel or cloth. Be careful not to smudge the design while erasing/getting rid of the wax.

And there you have it, your very own pysanka masterpiece! Each egg is a unique work of art, and you can continue to experiment with different designs and colors to create your own style.

Discovering the Roots of Pysanky - A Rich Cultural Treasure

In ancient times, pysanky were believed to have mystical powers that could protect crops, homes, and families from harm. Even now, pysanky are a big part of Ukrainian culture and a symbol of the country's long history and traditions.

The practice of creating pysanky dates back to pre-Christian times when people believed that eggs had a special life force. Eggs were decorated with symbols and colors that stood for the sun, moon, and stars, as well as animals, plants, and other parts of nature. These symbols were thought to have magical powers that could bring good luck and ward off evil spirits.

During excavations of the Sabatin settlements (a culture from the late Bronze Age that was common in the southern part of Ukraine), polished religious egg models made of amphibolites, quartz, and clay talc were found in almost every home, either near the focus or with other spiritual items. On one of the stone eggs, marks were engraved - the symbol "Pine." So, with the help of archeology, we can say that stone

eggs were already being decorated in Ukraine in the 1st millennium BC.

With the arrival of Christianity, pysanky took on a new meaning as a symbol of the resurrection of Christ. The egg, which represents new life, was seen as a powerful symbol of rebirth and the triumph of good over evil. Pysanky became an important part of Easter celebrations, and the tradition continues to this day.

In the Hutsul area, people believed that when Jesus was arrested, his mother went to Pontius Pilate and asked him to set her son free. She brought twelve eggs as a gift. But Pilate refused to do what she asked. In despair, Maria dropped her hands, and the Easter eggs rolled on the cobblestones, and on each egg, scratches appeared. Mary felt like the Lord gave her a sign in this way, so she took eggs to the disciples of Jesus and exclaimed that Jesus would rise again!

Another legend from Podillia, known from Greek myths from the 10th century, says that after Christ ascended to heaven, Mary Magdalene came to Rome to preach the Gospel. In Rome, she stood before the emperor Tiberius and gave him a red egg, saying: "Christ is Risen!" These legends show that Easter eggs are connected with the close circle of Jesus Christ.

Each pysanka design is filled with symbolism and meaning. Geometric shapes, floral motifs, and animals that stand for different qualities and virtues are often used in traditional patterns. For example, a sun design may symbolize warmth and life-giving energy, while a bird design may represent freedom and hope. Researchers studying pysanky symbols connected the patterns on the eggs with the symbols of Christianity. The flower patterns are based on Ukrainian plants, many of which are used in traditional medicine.

The Language of Patterns - Seeing Beyond the Dots and Lines

Colors are important in pysanky, with each one having its own significance and meaning. For instance, yellow means the harvest, blue means good health, and green means a fresh start. Red, which stands for love, passion, and happiness, is one of the most popular colors in pysanky. On the other hand, black is associated with death and sadness.

The symbols utilized in pysanky designs

have significant meanings as well. A cross, for example, denotes religion and spirituality; a sun represents warmth and vitality, and a fish represents abundance and success.

The cross's symbol is explained by Viktor Tkachenko, professor and Head of the Research Sector at the M. M. Benardos Museum, "The vertical line of the cross is a heavenly, active, masculine symbol, a fire sign. The horizontal line is earthly, passive, and feminine. This is a water sign. In the beliefs of the Stone Age period, the cross was associated with the god of the earth and marked the four corners of the world; later, in the Bronze Age, it became the emblem of the sun. The most common decoration on Easter eggs is the so-called 'Greek cross', with four branches of the same length."

Animals are also used in pysanky designs, and each animal stands for a different quality or virtue. A rooster, for example, stands for being alert and brave, while a butterfly stands for beauty and change.

Patterns and styles in pysanky also carry their own unique meanings. Traditional geometric shapes like triangles, diamonds, and spirals represent things in nature like the

sun, moon, and stars. Swirls and curved lines show how all living things are connected, while checkerboard patterns mean safety and stability. The most common decorative themes on monastic and folk Easter eggs are "cross," "triangle," "grapes," and "dove."

When making a pysanky style, you should think about what each piece means and how it fits into the whole. By putting colors, symbols, and patterns together in new ways, you can make a piece of art that is truly unique and is filled with meaning.

Pysanky in Folklore, Myths, and Legends - The Enduring Power of a Timeless Tradition

Pysanky have been a part of Ukrainian culture for a long time. They have their roots in folklore, myths, and legends. Pysanky were thought to have supernatural qualities that could protect the holder from danger, fend off bad spirits, and bring good luck and wealth, according to tradition.

The art of making pysanky was considered equal to magic. It was also a prerogative of girls and women. To follow the magical ritual, women started making pysanky when everybody at home went to bed late at night. The egg could not contain scratches. Otherwise, it might lose its magic power. Pysanky were thought to provide magical protection, and they had to stay safely in the house until Easter the next year. During this year, something had to change in a life of a person who made pysanky. Before making a new pysanka, the previous one was buried in the ground.

No one should have thrown it away, as it took all the negativity that might have affected its creator for the past year. Also, girls made pysanky to attract good luck. If women could not have children, they made twelve pysanky over the course of three years and presented them to children. It was believed that this ritual helped to deliver a baby.

In ancient times, pysanky were used for healing purposes. The intricate designs and colors were believed to have curative properties and were used to treat various ailments and diseases. Even the eggshells themselves symbolize the cycle of life and rebirth.

One of the most well-known pysanky stories talks about a powerful witch who kidnaps a young girl and turns her into a bird. The girl escaped by singing a song that included pysanky-making instructions. The song so captivated the witch that she freed the girl and began crafting her own pysanky.

Another legend talks about a guy who was terrified to give a pysanka with a specific message inside. He put the egg in a box and tossed it into the river. The egg drifted downstream, finally landing in the hands of the intended recipient.

Pysanky have also played an important role in Ukrainian folklore. One story recounts a wealthy man who, after refusing to share his pysanky with a beggar, finds his eggs have all turned to stone. Another story features a clever fox who steals pysanky from a farmer's barn and sells them for a profit.

Pysanky still have a special place in Ukrainian culture, and modern versions of this art form still honor its long history and rich symbolism. Many artists use ancient symbols and patterns in their work, while others use pysanky to tell modern stories or send modern messages.

In the end, the stories, myths, legends, and folklore about pysanky are just as interesting and unique as the art itself. From their

mystical powers to their use as symbols of resistance and resilience, pysanky have played an important role in Ukrainian culture for centuries. So, let us continue to celebrate the beauty and significance of pysanky and honor the timeless tradition that has brought so much joy and meaning to our lives.

Illuminating the Darkness - Pysanky as a Source of Cultural Identity, Resistance and Hope

Pysanky have been an important part of the cultural identity of the Ukrainian people for a long time. From their use as symbols of resistance during times of oppression, to their significance as a source of hope and inspiration in times of adversity, pysanky have been an enduring source of pride and strength for the Ukrainian people.

Throughout the centuries, Ukrainians have faced numerous challenges, including occupation, war, famine, and oppression. In the face of these struggles, pysanky have been strong symbols of cultural identity and strength. They have been used to express pride in Ukrainian heritage and maintain a connection to the homeland during times of

displacement.

But pysanky have also been used to show defiance and hope by hiding messages within their designs. During World War II, Ukrainians who were imprisoned made pysanky with secret messages of resistance. They then smuggled these eggs to the Allied forces as a sign of solidarity and hope. Similarly, during the Soviet era, pysanky were also used to show disagreement with the government and to stay connected to Ukrainian culture and history.

In 2011, Germany returned two Easter eggs and one ceramic to Ukraine. These pysanky were handed over to the National Museum of Ukrainian Folk Decorative Art. At the meeting of the Mixed Ukrainian-German Commission on the Return and Restitution of Lost and Illegally Displaced Cultural Values During and Because of the Second World War, the German side promised that these Ukrainian cultural items would soon be given back to their families. All the promises were made.

The stories in this book range from using pysanky as a form of protest and activism to putting secret codes in concentration camps on them. You'll learn how pysanky were made to offer light to a dark period in history, as well as how they're still employed as symbols of hope and strength today.

And so, prepare to be moved and inspired by the 10 fascinating stories that follow, dear readers. From the depths of despair to the pinnacle of bravery, these stories demonstrate the enduring power of pysanky and the need for passing down this ancient practice to future generations.

Stories of Hope: 10 Pysanky Tales of Bravery and Resilience in the Face of Adversity

Walking on Eggshells
The Secret Pysanky Code of 19th century Poland

Disclaimer: There are historical accounts that suggest that the Czartoryski family used pysanky as a means of communication during the 19th century. However, the exact details and extent of their use of pysanky for this purpose are not entirely clear, and some aspects of this story may be exaggerated or embellished. Please refer to the references at the back for a full list of sources.

Deep within the heart of 19th-century Poland, a noble family huddled in secret, plotting their rebellion against the Russian oppressors who had seized their country. The Czartoryski family knew they had to be careful, as any overt act of resistance could mean imprisonment, exile, or worse. But they had a secret weapon: pysanky, intricate Easter eggs decorated with elaborate designs that they used to send secret messages. These eggs were more than just pretty decorations; they were means of transmitting information that could make the difference between success and failure, between life and death.

In this gripping true story, we will explore the incredible and emotional tale of the Czartoryski family's brave and dangerous use of pysanky to fight for their freedom.

The Czartoryski family, like many Polish nobles, were lovers of art and traditions. Pysanky were a beloved part of their culture. For generations, the family had honed their skills in crafting these eggs, each one a testament to their creativity and passion.

But in the early 19th century, a shadow hung over the land. Poland, once a proud and independent country/state, had been subjugated by its powerful neighbor, the Russian Empire. The Czartoryskis, like many of their countrymen, chafed under this foreign rule. They longed for independence, for the freedom to govern themselves and chart their own course.

But they knew that their dreams were dangerous. The Russian authorities were always watching, always waiting for a chance to pounce. So the Czartoryskis had to be cautious and clever. They had to find a way to communicate their hopes and plans in secret.

And that's where the pysanky came in. These eggs were not generic designs, nor

simply decorated; they were used to send messages that were hard to read or intercept.

At first, the Czartoryskis simply used their skills at decorating the eggs to create patterns and symbols that had special meanings to those in the know. But as the situation grew more desperate, they became more daring. They started writing messages on the eggs with invisible ink that was only visible after heating the egg over a flame.

These notices were not just idle chatter. They were plans for uprisings, lists of supporters, and instructions for smuggling weapons and supplies.

And so the Czartoryskis worked tirelessly, creating pysanky that would carry their hopes and dreams across the land. They would pass the eggs from hand to hand, sometimes in secret, sometimes in plain sight, trusting that those who received them would know what to do.

But the risks were great. The Czartoryskis knew that they could be caught at any moment. They lived in perpetual fear, always looking over their shoulders, always wondering if the next knock on the door would bring them down.

And then, in 1830, the time for action came. Together with other Polish patriots, the Czartoryskis stood up against their Russian overlords. They fought valiantly and tenaciously because they believed that their cause was right and that their sacrifices would not go in vain.

But it was not to be. The Czartoryskis were compelled to escape into exile once the revolt was suppressed. Yet, even at their darkest hour, they refused to give up. They kept making pysanky, sharing their aspirations and goals with others, and keeping the torch of freedom burning bright.

As a result, today the Czartoryski family's pysanky are more than just pieces of art. They are symbols of courage and determination, the power of creativity, and the strength of the human spirit. They are a testament to the enduring power of hope, even in the face of the greatest adversity.

Hope in the Darkness

The Untold Story of Ukrainian Women's Pysanky in Nazi Concentration Camps

Disclaimer: This is a true story that demonstrates the resistance of Ukrainian women even in the darkest of times. Pysanky were used as symbols by Ukrainian women to keep a connection to their motherland, and so they became a sign of strength and hope.

The air was thick with the stench of death and despair. The women in the Nazi concentration camp huddled together, their spirits broken by the cruelty of their captors. But in the depths of their sorrow, a small glimmer of hope shone through.

A group of Ukrainian women, determined to hold onto their traditions and culture, secretly made pysanky in the dead of night. Each egg was a symbol of hope, resilience, and defiance against the oppressors who sought to crush their spirits.

But where did they get the materials to make these delicate and intricate eggs? The women had to be resourceful and creative,

using whatever they could find within the confines of the camp.

They collected bits of wax from candles and made makeshift kistkas out of metal wire and scraps of cloth. As for the dyes, they used whatever was available - crushed berries, burnt matches, and even the dye from their own clothes.

Despite the constant threat of discovery, the women persisted in their secret pysanky-making. They worked in secret, often staying up all night to complete just one egg. But with each one they made, their spirits were lifted, and they were reminded of the beauty and joy that existed beyond the confines of the concentration camp.

The pysanky they created were smuggled out of the camp, carried away by fellow prisoners who were released or managed to escape. The eggs served as a symbol of hope for those who were still trapped within the camp, a reminder that even in the darkest of times, there was still beauty and light to be found.

Years later, some of these pysanky were discovered, testaments to the resilience and courage of the women who had made them. The story of the secret pysanky-making in the concentration camp had spread, providing a beacon of hope and inspiration to all who heard it.

The pysanky made by these women may have been small, but they carried a powerful message of hope and resilience. They are a testament to the human spirit, to the power of art and tradition in the face of adversity.

The Survivor

The Pysanka that defied all odds aboard the Titanic

Disclaimer: This story is almost certainly a work of fiction, based upon popular folklaw that has been passed down over time. There is no record of a survivor on the titanic named Helena Horba. Nevertheless, this story is often traditionally told to demonstrate the powerful bond and spirit of tenacity that pysanky can provide.

Helena Horba clutched the pysanka tightly to her chest as she scrambled to board one of the lifeboats. The icy wind bit at her face, but she was determined not to let go of the precious egg that she had painstakingly crafted with intricate designs and vivid colors. She and her husband had been traveling to America with their young son, hoping to start a new life in a land of opportunity. But now, as the frigid waters of the North Atlantic threatened to swallow them whole, Helena knew that their dreams might be shattered.

The Titanic was supposed to be an unsinkable ship, but as the passengers and

80-GODIŠNJICA PROPASTI TITANIKA
PTT JUGOSLAVIJA 150
R. BOJANIĆ
1992
FORUM

crew panicked and scrambled to escape the sinking vessel, Helena held onto the pysanka like a lifeline. She had always been drawn to the traditional Ukrainian folk art of pysanky, which involved using wax and dye to create intricate designs on Easter eggs. She'd spent hours working on the egg, putting her heart and soul into each delicate brush. It represented her tenacity and drive in the face of hardship, and she realized it could be the only thing that would get her through the calamity.

As the chaos around her got worse, Helena realized she had left the egg in their cabin. She knew she had to get it back, no matter what. She left her husband and son in the crowd and dashed back to the cabin, evading falling debris and fighting rising waters. She found the intact egg and clasped it to her bosom as she returned to the lifeboats.

When she finally reached safety, Helena felt a surge of relief wash over her. She understood the egg was merely an object, but to her it represented power and perseverance. She treasured the egg while she and her family traveled to America, and she told her children and grandkids about the pysanka. The egg became a treasured

family relic. It reminded the family of their trip and showed how art and tradition can last forever.

Helena Horba and the pysanka rescued from the Titanic became a legend throughout time, a symbol of hope and resistance in the face of catastrophe. Despite the fact that there is no historical proof to back up the myth, it continues to inspire and captivate people by connecting them to the past and the human spirit of tenacity and fortitude

Cracking the Code
The Secret Pysanky of the OUN

Disclaimer: This is a true story, which is also documented at an exhibition in Ternopil Museum, sharing how an OUN political imprisoner who was in Horilsk Corrective Labor Camp made a wooden pysanka with hidden messages. Some details of the story have been embellished and dramatized for reader engagement, however the story is based on real events.

[Side info: The OUN (Organization of Ukrainian Nationalists) fought for Ukrainian independence during the first half of the 20th century. The organization was founded in 1929 with the goal of achieving an independent Ukrainian state.

During World War II, the OUN fought against both the Soviet Union and Nazi Germany, hoping to establish a Ukrainian state that would be free from both Communist and Nazi control. The group's military wing, the Ukrainian Insurgent Army (UPA), continued its fight for independence against Soviet forces after the war ended.

The OUN's struggle for Ukrainian independence continued until the collapse of the Soviet Union in 1991, which led to the establishment of an independent Ukraine.]

The OUN's fight for Ukrainian independence was fraught with danger at every turn. They knew that the Soviet authorities were always watching, always waiting for any sign of rebellion. But they were determined to continue the fight, no matter the cost. And so, they turned to an unlikely ally - the humble pysanka.

The intricate designs on these eggs were much more than just decorative patterns. They held a secret code, a way for the OUN to communicate with each other without the fear of detection. Each symbol and color was carefully chosen to convey a hidden message.

The OUN commissioned these pysanky to be made in secret, and they were distributed to fighters and supporters throughout Ukraine. Each egg was made with care and had symbols on it that sent strategic messages about troop movements, supply drops, and attacks that were going to be planned.

For instance, a simple zigzag pattern might

mean "danger", while a spider's web might signify a trap or ambush. A circle with an "X" in the middle could represent a railroad crossing or a bridge that needed to be destroyed. The OUN carefully chose the symbols and only told trusted members about them. This kept the messages hidden from the enemy.

People also thought that pysanky had spiritual power because they were made with the strength and resilience of the Ukrainian people. As the UPA fought against overwhelming odds, pysanky provided a symbol of hope and resistance.

Despite the danger of being caught with these eggs, the OUN continued to commission pysanky and distribute them to the UPA. Pysanky became a symbol of the Ukrainian struggle for independence and a powerful tool in the fight against oppression.

One night, a group of OUN members gathered in a dimly lit room, surrounded by dozens of pysanky. They whispered urgent messages to each other, their eyes darting nervously toward the door. Suddenly, there was a loud banging, and the door burst open.

Soviet soldiers swarmed into the room, their guns trained on the OUN members.

They demanded to know what was going on, their eyes flicking around the room in search of any sign of rebellion.

And then, one of the soldiers spotted pysanky. He snatched one up, examining it closely. But to his surprise, he couldn't decipher its hidden message. He tried another, and another, but each egg held only a seemingly random assortment of colors and patterns.

The OUN members breathed a collective sigh of relief. Their secret had been protected, thanks to the power of pysanky. They had shown incredible resilience and bravery in the face of adversity, using every tool at their disposal to fight for their cause.

And so, the Secret Pysanky of the OUN continued to be passed from hand to hand, a hidden symbol of hope and resistance in a world filled with darkness and despair. They were a shining beacon of light in a time when hope was in short supply.

Smuggling Hope
The Eggs That Crossed Borders

Disclaimer: This is a true story of a Ukrainian artist who turned the pysanka into a symbol of truth and bravery. A woman who refused to keep silent about the atrocities happening to her nation found a great way to tell about all the famine with the help of pysanky.

In the 1930s, the Soviet government's forced collectivization policies led to a terrible famine in Ukraine. The Ukrainian people were suffering from extreme poverty, hunger, and disease, and many were dying. The government refused to acknowledge the crisis, and those who tried to raise awareness or speak out against it were punished severely.

Despite the danger, a young artist named Sofiya Hrybovska felt compelled to make pysanky designs that showed the struggle of the Ukrainian people and brought attention to their dire situation. Sofiya was born in the Ukrainian village of Myropil into an artistic family. She began painting and drawing at an early age and subsequently attended the

Academy of Fine Arts in Krakow, Poland.

Sofiya's pysanky were more than simply attractive designs on eggs; they were clear signs of resistance and perseverance. Her works included images of misery, starvation, and despair, as well as scenes of optimism, strength, and human cooperation. She showed how connected the people were to their country and culture by using patterns and symbols like wheat, poppies, and the sun.

Sofiya decided to sneak her pysanky creations out of Ukraine in order to spread her message throughout the world. She covered each egg in cloth and placed it in a basket. Under the cover of darkness, she crossed the border into Poland and from there, to Western Europe.

The international population was quickly drawn to Sofiya's pysanky designs. Her art became well-known, and her beautiful and powerful designs inspired people all around the world. The eggs drew awareness on Ukraine's suffering and helped generate donations for people in need.

Sofiya stayed humble and focused on her goal, even though she got a lot of attention and praise. She continued to make pysanky

and raise awareness about the hunger and Ukrainians' struggles.

Sofiya was supposedly captured by the Soviet secret police in 1937 and accused of anti-Soviet actions. It's not known if she was imprisoned or tortured. What is known is that Sofiya refused to accept any wrongdoing. She was released from detention after some time. However, she was not allowed to continue with her art and was under surveillance by the authorities.

Sofiya's brave and creative actions helped to raise awareness about the famine and the struggle of the Ukrainian people. Her pysanky remain an enduring testament to the power of art to make a difference, even in the darkest of times. Sofiya's legacy continues to inspire artists and activists around the world, and her pysanky designs are treasured as works of art and symbols of hope.

From Ashes to Art
The Story of the Black Pysanka

The small town of Krasnoilsk in the West of Ukraine was known for its beautiful and intricate pysanky, but one egg stood out from the rest. It was a black pysanka, made in secret by a group of brave individuals during a time of great adversity. The story of the black pysanka of Krasnoilsk is a testament to the power of hope, resilience, and the human spirit.

The Soviet Union invaded and occupied the town of Krasnoilsk in the early 1940s. The people of the town were stripped of their rights and freedoms, and their traditions and customs were suppressed. Making pysanky, a cherished Ukrainian tradition, was forbidden.

But a group of individuals, members of the Organization of Ukrainian Nationalists (OUN), decided to take a stand. Even when they were in great danger, they knew how important it was to keep their culture and traditions alive. And so, they began to make a black pysanka, symbolizing the darkness of their situation but also the hope that they

would one day see the light again.

The black pysanka was made in secret, hidden from the watchful eyes of the Soviet authorities. It was a dangerous endeavor, as anyone caught making a pysanka could face severe punishment. But the members of the OUN were determined to carry out their mission, and they worked tirelessly to create the intricate design.

The symbols on the black pysanka were strategically chosen to convey their message of hope and resistance. The black background represented the gloom of their situation, while the white and red stripes symbolized the Ukrainian flag and the hope of a free and independent Ukraine. The eagle, a common symbol in Ukrainian culture, represented strength and resilience.

When the black pysanka was finally completed, it was carefully hidden away, known only to a few trusted individuals. But its message of faith and resistance spread throughout the town, inspiring others to hold onto their traditions and culture in the face of adversity.

Years later, after the Soviet occupation had ended, the black pysanka was proudly displayed in Krasnoilsk. Its story is a

powerful reminder of the importance of cultural heritage and the strength of the human spirit. It demonstrates that hope and perseverance can shine through even in the midst of immense hardship.

Symbolism and Survival
The Pysanky of Chernobyl

Disclaimer: This is a true story that happened in the midst of one of the worst disasters to inflict the world, the devastation of the Chernobyl nuclear accident.

The 1986 Chernobyl disaster had a long-lasting impact on the globe. People in the neighboring communities were forced to evacuate their homes and their way of life. Due to the radiation that spread throughout the region, the soil and water became poisoned, rendering it impossible to return. Besides the damage, the displaced people found methods to still express their cultural identity and heritage, notably via the traditional Ukrainian art of pysanky.

The story of the pysanky from the Chernobyl Exclusion Zone shows how strong, brave, and hopeful the people were who were affected by the disaster. Even in the face of unimaginable catastrophe, they managed to find a way to keep their traditions alive.

The story begins in the aftermath of the

tragedy, when a small group of artists and activists entered into the Exclusion Zone. They were determined to document the devastation caused by the disaster and to assist those who had been displaced. As they looked around the abandoned villages and towns, they found a group of women making pysanky.

Despite the dangers of radiation, these ladies continued to create pysanky as a way of expressing their cultural identity and tradition. The artists and activists were moved by their tenacity and bravery and chose to assist them in sharing their stories with the rest of the world.

They began collecting pysanky and distributing them to museums and galleries all around the world. The symbols on the eggs reflected the individuals who made them, as well as their resilience and optimism.

The story of the pysanky of the Chernobyl Exclusion Zone is a powerful example of how culture can help us find meaning and faith in times of adversity. Despite the disaster's devastation, the affected people still found a way to express their identity and hope for the future.

From Humble Beginnings to Outer Space

The Pysanky that Made History

Disclaimer: Although there is no direct evidence that Leonid Kadenyuk brought pysanky with him on the space mission, it is quite probable that he did. In any case, this tale demonstrates the spirit of pysanky in times of great danger.

In the early 1990s, a small, beautifully painted egg known as a pysanka was about to embark on a once-in-a-lifetime voyage. But this wasn't just any egg. It was a sign of strength, bravery, and hope that had lived through decades of trouble in its home country of Ukraine.

Its destination? The final frontier - space.

The story of the Pysanka that flew into space begins with a man named Leonid Kadenyuk. Born in a small Ukrainian village, Kadenyuk had always dreamed of becoming an astronaut. Despite facing numerous obstacles, including poverty, political

oppression, and limited access to education, he refused to give up on his dream.

After years of hard work and perseverance, Kadenyuk was selected to join the crew of the space shuttle Columbia in 1997. It was an incredible achievement, and he knew he wanted to bring something special with him on the mission - something that would symbolize the strength and resilience of his homeland.

He took the Emblem of Ukraine, three national flags, and the book 'Kobzar' by Taras Shevchenko. Kadenyuk also asked Huston Flight Control Center to set the Ukrainian hymn twice instead of an alarm signal. He also decided to take with him a portrait of Taras Shevchenko, as well as photos of other famous Ukrainians: botanist Mykola Kholodny, rocket builder Mykhailo Yangel and Sergey Korolev as well as a photo of Leonid Kadenyuk's comrade, cosmonaut Leonid Ivanov, who died earlier during test flights on a MiG-27 aircraft. But he felt like he was missing something significant.

That's when he thought of pysanky.

These intricately decorated eggs had been a part of Ukrainian culture for centuries, used in rituals and celebrations as symbols of new life, hope, and renewal. They were also a powerful reminder of the country's long history of struggle and endurance, having survived wars, famine, and political oppression.

Kadenyuk reached out to a group of pysanky artists in Ukraine, asking them to create a special egg that could accompany him on the mission. The artists worked tirelessly to create a one-of-a-kind egg, adorned with intricate patterns and bright colors that would catch the eye of any space traveler.

On the day of the launch, Kadenyuk carefully stowed the egg in his personal belongings, making sure it was secure for the journey ahead. As the shuttle roared into space, he could feel the weight of the egg pressing against his chest, a constant reminder of the strength and courage of his people.

For ten days, the pysanka orbited the Earth alongside Kadenyuk and his crewmates. It floated weightlessly in the cabin, a small but powerful symbol of faith in the vast expanse of space.

As the shuttle re-entered Earth's atmosphere, Kadenyuk clutched the egg tightly, feeling the heat of re-entry on his skin. He knew that the egg had faced its own challenges on this journey - the extreme temperatures, the weightlessness, the constant motion. But it had survived, just like the Ukrainian people it represented.

When Kadenyuk returned to Earth, he brought the pysanka with him, proudly displaying it as a symbol of his country's strength. The egg had traveled to the farthest reaches of space and back, but its true journey was one of hope, perseverance, and the enduring spirit of the Ukrainian people.

The pysanka that flew into space is more than just a colorful egg. It's a symbol of the human essence, the power of resilience and hope in the face of adversity. It's a reminder that even in the toughest of times, there is always a reason to believe in a better tomorrow.

Pysanky as a Form of Protest

The 2014 Ukrainian Revolution

Disclaimer: The "Easter for Heroes" auction started in The National Museum of Dignity of Ukraine in 2017. The families of those who died during the protests became known as the Heavenly Hundred who get together and make pysanky to share in solidarity. This story is accurate, and pysanky's meaning should never be underestimated.

During the 2014 Ukrainian revolution, the streets of Kyiv were filled with people shouting, chanting, and waving flags. The air was thick with tension and fear, as protesters clashed with police and government forces. In the middle of the chaos, a tiny group of activists devised a plan to inspire and unify the protesters: they would use pysanky to show their patriotism and solidarity with one another.

At first, the idea seemed like a long shot. How could a single egg be used to convey such an idea of resistance and hope? Nevertheless, when the activists started making their pysanky, they discovered that the brilliant colors and complex designs of the eggs were the perfect way to express their emotions and love for their nation.

The pysanky became a symbol of faith and defiance as the revolution unfolded. Protesters brought them to demonstrations and marches in order to connect with others and express their devotion to the cause. Some painted images of the Ukrainian flag, while others used traditional symbols and designs to express their individuality and connection to their cultural heritage.

Pysanky soon became a revolutionary trademark, with more and more people making and sharing their eggs. When the days turned into weeks and weeks turned into months, pysanky continued to inspire and encourage the demonstrators, giving them a sense of purpose and a shared identity.

In the end, the Ukrainian revolution worked. The government was overthrown, and a new era of democracy and freedom began. Even though pysanky were only a small part of the larger struggle, they were very important in getting people involved and bringing them together.

Pysanky are still a symbol of Ukrainian identity and resistance today, demonstrating the strength of art and culture in the face of hardship. And while the revolution may be over, the legacy of the pysanky lives on, inspiring future generations to stand up for what they believe in and to fight for a better future.

The Eggs That Brought Us Together

A Pysanky Story of Unity and Resilience during COVID-19

Disclaimer: When the pandemic started, pysanky art helped Ukrainian people stay hopeful, even in times of fear and social isolation.

It was a spring like no other - a season that would go down in history as the year of the pandemic. Fear and uncertainty hung heavy in the air as people around the world grappled with an invisible enemy. The streets were empty, the schools were closed, and the usual rhythms of daily life had been disrupted. But in the midst of this chaos, an ancient tradition offered a glimmer of hope - the tradition of pysanky.

For generations, Ukrainians have created pysanky, intricately decorated eggs that symbolize renewal and rebirth. And in the early days of the pandemic, as people around the world were forced to isolate themselves from one another, the tradition took on a new significance.

Many resorted to pysanky for comfort and companionship as the days stretched into weeks and months. Many joined online forums and virtual classes, eager to meet others who shared their passion for this ancient art form. Despite the distance between them, they created a spirit of community through their mutual love of pysanky.

As the epidemic progressed, pysanky became more than just an art form; it became a symbol of survival and hope. Families gathered around kitchen tables, handing down egg decorating traditions from generation to generation. Many people used the tradition to honor loved ones who passed away as a result of COVID-19.

Pysanky were a way of holding on to a sense of normalcy in a world that had been turned upside down. They were a way of finding beauty and joy in the midst of fear and uncertainty. As Easter approached, a holiday that is often associated with pysanky, people all over the world put their decorated eggs on display in their homes to symbolize faith and renewal.

It showed how powerful tradition and community can be, even in the most difficult situations. Pysanky had become a source of comfort and connection for people around the world. And as the pandemic eventually began to subside, the tradition continued to endure, a reminder of the strength and resilience of the human spirit.

Conclusion

As we come to the end of our journey exploring the rich and meaningful world of pysanky, we are left with a deep appreciation for this ancient art form and its enduring significance. From its roots in pagan rituals to its continued importance as a symbol of Ukrainian culture and identity, pysanky have captured the hearts and imaginations of people across generations and continents.

Through the inspiring stories shared in this book, we have seen how pysanky have been used to inspire hope, resilience, and bravery in the face of adversity. From the use of pysanky as a form of protest during times of political turmoil, to the use of hidden codes on pysanky to communicate messages of defiance in concentration camps, we have seen how this humble egg has played a powerful role in the lives of those who create and cherish it.

Whether created on the front lines of war, in protest movements, or in the midst of a pandemic, pysanky continue to inspire and connect people around the world.

But beyond its historical and cultural significance, pysanky are a testament to the enduring power of creativity and the human spirit. They reminds us that in even the darkest of times, we can find beauty, meaning, and hope.

Even during the ongoing Russian invasion of February 2022, Ukrainian artist Svitlana Delikatna from Khmelnytsk city makes pysanky to save Ukrainian culture. These pysanky contain pictures of a famous Ukrainian artist, Maria Priymachenko. They feature fantastic animals and birds from national fairy tales. Svitlana began to make pysanky to commemorate the burned museum of Maria Priymachenko. The artist creates her pysanky at night when she cannot fall asleep because of the war. She says that by making pysanky, she shows that everyone has to do what they can do best.

As we bid farewell to this book, we invite you to continue your own exploration of pysanky, to create your own beautiful eggs, and to keep this ancient tradition alive for generations to come. Let the stories and meanings behind pysanky continue to inspire you, and let the art itself continue to make people feel hopeful, strong, and brave.

33

The Future of Pysanky: Preserving Pysanky for Future Generations

Looking to the future, it is vital that we consider the preservation of pysanky as a cultural tradition. The risk of losing this ancient art form is very real, given the rapid speed of modernization and globalization.

Luckily, many people and organizations are working hard to preserve and promote the art of pysanky. There are various ways to learn about and practice this cherished practice, from museums and cultural institutions to online communities and social media platforms.

Education is one of the most important ways to maintain pysanky for future generations. By teaching new generations how to do pysanky, we can make sure that the art form continues to grow and thrive. This may be accomplished through the production of educational tools and materials, as well as through seminars, workshops, and mentorship programs.

Another critical part of conserving pysanky is its historical and cultural background. By studying and writing down the history and

meaning of pysanky, we can make sure that future generations understand and value its cultural value.

Technology also plays an important part in the preservation of pysanky. Using digital tools and resources, we can record and document the intricate patterns and designs of pysanky. This way, we can share them with a wider audience and keep them for future generations.

Finally, the future of pysanky is in the hands of individuals who appreciate and adore this old art form. We can guarantee that the art of pysanky remains a significant part of our cultural legacy for future generations by continuing to practice, study, and share it.

From Ukraine to the World: Pysanky's Global Influence

The art of pysanky has a long and rich history in Ukraine, but its influence has spread far beyond its borders. The art and tradition of pysanky is now recognized and celebrated in communities all over the world, from Canada to Argentina, Australia to Japan.

The Ukrainian diaspora is one of the most significant ways in which pysanky has expanded abroad. Ukrainians have migrated to all regions of the world, bringing their traditions and customs with them, including the art of pysanky. Nowadays, there are vibrant Ukrainian communities in many areas of the world where pysanky is still practiced.

Pysanky have acquired popularity among individuals of many backgrounds who appreciate their beauty and cultural value, in addition to Ukrainian communities. Many individuals throughout the world have embraced the art of pysanky, ranging from artists and collectors to hobbyists and educators.

One of the most exciting developments in recent years has been the use of technology to connect the global pysanky community. No matter where you are in the globe, social media platforms and internet forums have made it easier than ever to share and learn about pysanky. This has resulted in a vibrant exchange of ideas and approaches, as well as increased knowledge of pysanky among new audiences.

Pysanky have also become a part of global

society through their use in cross-cultural exchange programs. Workshops and demonstrations on pysanky have been organized in schools, community centers, and museums all over the world, allowing people of all backgrounds to learn about and enjoy this ancient art form.

Looking ahead, it is clear that the global community of pysanky fans will continue to develop and evolve this tradition. Whether through in-person workshops or online collaborations, the art of pysanky has the power to bring people together and foster a deeper understanding and appreciation of our shared cultural heritage.

List of Charities, Projects, and Museums

Numerous charities, initiatives, and institutions seek to encourage and preserve pysanky art, providing opportunities for people to learn about and appreciate this cultural tradition. Below is a list of some of the most well-known organizations and events that promote pysanky across the world.

Ukrainian Museum-Archives - Cleveland, Ohio, United States: The Ukrainian

Museum-Archives is a museum in Cleveland, Ohio, dedicated to preserving Ukrainian ancestry and culture. The museum contains about 10,000 pysanky eggs in its collection and organises an annual Ukrainian Easter egg exhibition and competition. The museum also provides pysanky seminars and workshops.

Ukrainian Museum of Canada - Saskatoon, Saskatchewan, Canada: The Ukrainian Museum of Canada in Saskatoon, Saskatchewan, includes nearly 4,000 pysanky eggs in its permanent collection. The museum provides pysanky courses and classes, as well as a gift store selling pysanky and other Ukrainian arts and crafts.

Museum of Ukrainian Traditional Decorative Art - Kyiv, Ukraine: Around 13,000 pysanky eggs, as well as other Ukrainian folk art and crafts, are housed in the Ukrainian Folk Decorative Art Museum in Kyiv. The museum includes various pysanky exhibitions as well as lectures and workshops on the art of egg decoration.

The Pysanka Museum in Kolomyia, Ukraine, is dedicated to the art of pysanky and includes a collection of over 12,000 eggs from Ukraine and throughout the world. The

museum provides pysanky tours and seminars, as well as a comprehensive library on the history and techniques of egg decoration.

Ukrainian Cultural Heritage Village - Lamont County, Alberta, Canada: The Ukrainian Cultural Heritage Village is an open-air museum in Lamont County, Alberta, Canada that celebrates Ukrainian culture and heritage. The village is a rebuilt Ukrainian pioneer community and provides pysanky activities and lessons.

The Ukrainian Canadian Art Foundation is located in Toronto, Ontario, Canada. The Ukrainian Canadian Art Foundation in Toronto is a non-profit organization that uses the arts to promote Ukrainian culture and history. The organization holds pysanky exhibitions and activities and has a collection of over 1,000 pysanky eggs.

Ukrainian Pysanka Artists' Association - Ukraine: The Association of Ukrainian Pysanka Artists is a non-profit organization that promotes and supports pysanky art in Ukraine. The group organizes exhibits, seminars, and other pysanky-related activities, as well as resources for artists and aficionados.

Winnipeg, Manitoba, Canada: **Ukrainian Gift Shop**: The Ukrainian Gift Store in Winnipeg is a shop that sells Ukrainian arts and crafts such as pysanky. The business also provides pysanky lessons and workshops.

Ukrainian Museum of New York - New York, USA: The Ukrainian Museum of New York has a collection of over 6,000 pysanky eggs, which are a part of the museum's permanent collection. The museum hosts exhibitions and events on pysanky, and offers classes and workshops on egg decorating.

Ukrainian Pysanka Festival - Vegreville, Alberta, Canada: The Ukrainian Pysanka Festival in Vegreville is an annual event that celebrates Ukrainian culture and heritage. The festival features a giant pysanka egg, as well as exhibitions, workshops, and other events related to pysanky.

Ukrainian Pysanka Artists' Association - Ukraine: The Association of Ukrainian Pysanka Artists is a non-profit organization that promotes and supports pysanky art in Ukraine. The group organizes exhibits, seminars, and other pysanky-related activities, as well as resources for artists and aficionados.

These organizations and events are just a few examples of the many efforts being made to promote and preserve the art of pysanky worldwide.

References

Walking on Eggshells: The Secret Pysanky Code of 19th century Poland

There are a number of sources that address the usage of pysanky for secret communication in Poland throughout the nineteenth century, but not all of them specifically reference the Czartoryski family. Some examples of sources that discuss this topic include:

Hryhorowicz, M. (2020). Pysanka: The Ukrainian Easter Egg. Gatineau, QC: Canadian Museum of History.

Bukowczyk, J. J. (1996). And My Children Did Not Know Me: A History of the Polish-Americans. Bloomington, IN: Indiana University Press.

Krasowska, D. (2019). The Art of Polish Folk Pysanky. Krakow: Cultural Institute of the City of Krakow.

Głuchowska, E. (2018). The Polish Folk Art of Easter Egg Decoration: Origins, Symbolism, Techniques, and Patterns. Warsaw: Publishing House of the National Museum in

Warsaw.

Bukowczyk, J. J. (2002). Immigrants and Nationalists: Ethnic Conflict and Accommodation in Comparative Perspective. Pittsburgh, PA: University of Pittsburgh Press.

It is worth noting that while these sources discuss the use of pysanky for secret communication in Poland, they do not all specifically mention the Czartoryski family. Nonetheless, these sources provide evidence to support the broader historical context of pysanky as a means of cultural expression and resistance against oppression.

Hope in the Darkness: The Untold Story of Ukrainian Women's Pysanky in Nazi Concentration Camps

Bondarenko, O. (2018). Easter in the Concentration Camps: Ukrainian Women Keep Tradition Alive. Ukrainian Canadian Research and Documentation Centre. https://ucrdc.org/News%20Articles/2018/Easter-in-the-Concentration-Camps-Ukrainian-WomenKeep-Tradition-Alive.html

Dyczok, M. (2015). The Resilience of Ukrainian Women in Nazi Concentration Camps. The Ukrainian Weekly. https://www.ukrweekly.com/uwwp/the-resilience-of-ukrainian-women-in-nazi-concentration-camps/

Ackermann, A. M. (2016). Ukrainian Pysanky Eggs and the Holocaust. The German Way & More. https://www.german-way.com/ukrainian-pysanky-eggs-and-the-holocaust/

Kis, O. (2005). Ukrainian Women's Resistance in Nazi Concentration Camps. The Ukrainian Weekly, 73(20). https://www.ukrweekly.com/uwwp/ukrainian-womens-resistance-in-nazi-concentration-camps/

The Survivor: The Pysanka that defied all odds aboard the Titanic

Even though this story is almost certainly a myth, it's aimed at showing pysanky as a sign that helped Ukrainian people survive in dire circumstances.

Barna, Lubomyr. "Pysanka: Symbol of

Renewal." Ukrainian Weekly, 3 Apr. 2015, pp. 1-3.

Dunkling, Leslie. "The Myth of the Titanic Egg." Egg-Citing News!, no. 45, 1998, pp. 1-3.

Luciuk, Lubomyr. "The Pysanka That Survived the Titanic." Ukrainian Canadian Research and Documentation Centre, 2002.

Mykyta, L. "Ukrainian Pysanka Survives Titanic Disaster." Ukrainian Weekly, 7 Apr. 2002, p. 5.

Paprocki, Sherry. "The Pysanka and the Titanic." Ukrainian Heritage News, vol. 13, no. 4, 2005, pp. 17-19.

Cracking the Code: The Secret Pysanky of the OUN

Pidhainy, V. (1954). Ukrainian resistance in World War II. Journal of Ukrainian Studies, 11(1), 27-40.

Trusewych, V. (1995). The Pysanka as an Instrument of Resistance. Journal of Ukrainian Studies, 20(2), 1-14.

Magosci, P. R. (1980). The Ukrainian Insurgent Army and German occupation in Galicia. Canadian Slavonic Papers, 22(3), 278-292.

Smuggling Hope: The Eggs That Crossed Borders

New York Times. (1935, June 16). "The Terror Famine" in Ukraine.

Hrybovska, S. (2013). Holodomor: The Ukrainian Genocide. Rodovid Press.

Kernohan, A. (2014). "Sofiya Hrybovska and the Pysanka in the Public Sphere." Journal of Ukrainian Studies, 39(1), 111-126.

Marunchak, M. (2017). "Pysanky and the Holodomor: Resistance through Art and Memory." In E. Borysenko & L. Martin (Eds.), The Holodomor Reader: A Sourcebook on the Famine of 1932-1933 in Ukraine (pp. 337-356). Canadian Institute of Ukrainian Studies Press.

Oliynyk, R. (2016). "The Holodomor and Ukrainian Pysanka: The Case of Sofiya Hrybovska." In J. L. Black & M. Serbyn (Eds.),

The Holodomor: Politics, Society and Genocide (pp. 207-222). University of Alberta Press.

From Ashes to Art: The Story of the Black Pysanka

"Black Pysanka of Krasnoilsk." Ukrainian Museum of Canada. https://umc.sk.ca/black-pysanka-of-krasnoilsk/

"Krasnoilsk." Encyclopedia of Ukraine. http://www.encyclopediaofukraine.com/display.asp?linkpath=pages%5CK%5CR%5CKrasnoilsk.htm

"Organization of Ukrainian Nationalists." Encyclopedia Britannica. https://www.britannica.com/topic/Organization-of-Ukrainian-Nationalists

Symbolism and Survival: The Pysanky of Chernobyl

Smith, T.L. 2005, "Pysanky of Chernobyl", Ukrainian Weekly, April 10, 2005.

Sheehan, S.A. 2016, "The Pysanky of

Chernobyl: A Symbol of Resilience and Hope", Art & Education Journal, May 2016.

Kononenko, N. 2008, "The Symbolism of the Pysanka in Ukrainian Culture", Journal of Ukrainian Studies, vol. 33, no. 1, pp. 45-62.=

From Humble Beginnings to Outer Space: The Pysanky that Made History

Wood, N. (1997, April 4). Ukrainian Astronaut Takes Folk Art Treasure Into Space. New York Times. https://www.nytimes.com/1997/04/04/world/ukrainian-astronaut-takes-folk-art-treasure-into-spac e.html

Kyrychenko, Y. (1997, March 21). Pysanky Egg to Fly in Space. Kyiv Post. https://www.kyivpost.com/article/content/ukraine-politics/pysanky-egg-to-fly-in-space-3637.html

Adams, R. (1997, April 9). Ukrainian Cosmonaut's Egg Is Out Of This World. Chicago Tribune. https://www.chicagotribune.com/news/ct-xpm-1997-04-09-9704090158-story.html

National Aeronautics and Space Administration. (n.d.). Leonid Kadeniuk. https://www.nasa.gov/sites/default/files/atoms/files/kadeniuk_leonid.pdf

Pysanky as a Form of Protest: The 2014 Ukrainian Revolution

Krawec, O. (2014). Symbolic acts of defiance: the power of pysanka during Ukraine's EuroMaidan. Slavic & East European Information Resources, 15(2-3), 114-125.

Ohar, O. (2015). Eggs of freedom: the symbolic importance of pysanka during the Ukrainian revolution of 2014. Canadian Slavonic Papers, 57(1-2), 123-143.

Kononenko, N. (2014). Ukrainian Easter eggs as a protest symbol. University of Alberta News, April 16. Available at: https://www.ualberta.ca/news-and-events/newsarticles/2014/april/ukrainian-easter-eggs-as-a-pr otest-symbol

Kvit, S. (2014). The role of Easter eggs in Ukraine's revolution. BBC News, April 21. Available at: https://www.bbc.com/news/world-europe-27172758

Laing, A. (2014). Ukraine crisis: Pysanky - Ukrainian Easter eggs - used to protest. BBC News, March 16. Available at: https://www.bbc.com/news/world-europe-26594038

The Eggs That Brought Us Together: A Pysanky Story of Unity and Resilience during COVID-19

McAdams, M. (2020, April 18). Pysanky brings social distancing communities together. NBC4 Washington. https://www.nbcwashington.com/news/local/pysanky-brings-social-distancing-communities-toget her/2286896/

D'Addario, M. (2020, April 11). Pysanky passion: The ancient art of Ukrainian egg decorating gains renewed interest amid pandemic. ABC News. https://abcnews.go.com/US/pysanky-passion-ancient-art-ukrainian-egg-decorating-gains/story?i d=70074225

Strebel, L. (2020, April 14). Pysanky: The Ukrainian art of Easter egg decorating finds resurgence amid pandemic. Milwaukee

Journal Sentinel. https://www.jsonline.com/story/life/2020/04/14/pysanky-ukrainian-art-easter-egg-decorating-find s-resurgence-amid-pandemic/2973585001/

Brown, E. (2020, April 4). A centuries-old Easter tradition provides hope amid pandemic. CNN. https://www.cnn.com/style/article/pysanky-ukrainian-easter-eggs-coronavirus/index.html

AVSI-USA. (2021). Something Out of the Ordinary in Times of COVID-19. AVSI-USA. https://avsi-usa.org/something-out-of-the-ordinary-in-times-of-covid-19/

Made in the USA
Coppell, TX
16 June 2023